# *Icon Driven*

Poems by Eric Folsom

Wolsak and Wynn • Toronto

Typeset in Arial.
Printed in Canada by The Coach House Printing Company, Toronto.

Front cover art: Don Maynard
Cover Design: The Coach House
Author's photograph: Colleen Richardson

The publisher and the author gratefully acknowledge the Canada Council for the Arts and the Ontario Arts Council for their generous support.

The Canada Council for the Arts | Le Conseil des Arts du Canada

ONTARIO ARTS COUNCIL
CONSEIL DES ARTS DE L'ONTARIO

Versions of "Jack Pine" appeared in *Modern Fuel* newsletter and in the Foxglove/Beach Holme anthology *On the Threshold*. "Ain't no more in this world" was a broadside for the TREE Reading Series from rob mclennan's above/ground press. A version of "She had twentieth-dynasty eyes" was published as "The woman with Minoan eyes" in the Mercury/League of Canadian Poets anthology, *More Garden Varieties Two*. *Arc* published "War."

The author would like to acknowledge his gratitude to *Arc* and to the Banff Centre for the Arts, and extends a big thank you to everyone at Banff's 1997 Writing Studio, and also to Mary Cameron, Allan Brown, Steven Heighton, Brenda Fuhrman, and Don McKay. The performance text of "Mixed at Scream/Mixed at Bad Animals" incorporates suggestions from Don McKay, Sina Queyras, and Kathy Mac. Last, but never least, major gratitude to Diane Schoemperlen for saying, "You ought to write that!"

Wolsak and Wynn Publishers Ltd, 192 Spadina Ave, Ste 315, Toronto, ON, M5T 2C2

National Library of Canada Cataloguing in Publication Data

Folsom, Eric, 1951-
    Icon Driven

Poems.
ISBN 0-919897-72-x

I. Title

PS8561.O48I26 2001    C811'.54    C2001-930592-3
PR9199.3.F64I26 2001

*This book is for my parents, Allan and Helen Folsom*

*The emperor* ***is*** *wherever his effigies are. The saint is said to be mystically present in her icons, which do not accordingly merely depict her: they bring her into our midst. Since the emperor or saint is present, the images in which he or she is so are not required to resemble their subjects, any more than a saint must resemble the relic in which he is embodied.*

—Arthur C. Danto, *Beyond the Brillo Box*

*Plainly we are dealing with materials distorted from their original form.*
—Jack Spicer, "The Holy Grail"

*what he had forgotten:*
*actual*
*thinkable things cling*
*to the unthinkable*

—Robin Blaser, "Image-Nation 7 (l'air"

# Contents

## o / The jack pine

everything had a shape
every shape had a place and a texture

    strokes of green, apricot, indigo
    generous helpings of raw paint
    going up against real rock, cold water

as in "Spring Thaw" and "In The Northland"
Tom Thomson used the brush like an axe
to shape the trees, recast the land

    precision (so many of the Seven
    worked weekdays as graphic artists
    their hands shaped by Grip Ltd)
    colour, composition and light

the brush/stroke of fate that was Tom's accident
a waterlogged body dragged from Canoe Lake
anonymously, quietly, *nature morte*

    the later Jack Pines were painted and pruned
    Varley's feathery charmer, Lismer's sculpted
    pine sentinel four-square in the rocks

the style was set, outlines positioned
colours chosen and textures applied
    across the region like commercial animation
    or settlers creating a space, then filling it in
        thousands of public schools later
        paintings raised to icon status
        brush/strokes fading to official image

show me the photograph of Tom fishing
    could be your own lost brother or uncle
        (observe old coyote slipping behind a tree)
show me the rough shed where Tom lived and worked
        down behind Severn Street in Toronto

mere spitting distance from the Studio Building
where others of the Seven had light, airy workspace
bankrolled by Harris and Dr McCallum
young bush-mad Tom, perpetually out of cash
slept rough, whenever he wanted, and painted
in a self-made shack half-hidden by a leaning fence

we might see him there still, feeding broken sticks
rejected sketches, bits of the future
into the flame of an old Quebec heater

## 1 / Style

sired of dark Slovakian mountains and Pittsburgh slag
    drawn to drawing and the midnight money of New York
photomorphic improviser looking to catch light
        with cameras, reflective mylar balloons
    Brillo bright, the supremely desirable world
        and Andy almost wordlessly
        black turtleneck, dark glasses
        black jeans
        white wig

Jean Baudrillard would have you think
    of the emptiness, the way meaning is
        always and permanently deflected
    of superficiality, the reproduced image
        something beyond art
        in the age of no content
    Andy so far beyond alienation
        he received a purified joy

but think of Warhol as Manhattan's Cocteau
        an almost Cocteau, a would-be dandy
    picture him aspiring to the den of iniquity
        it wasn't just about getting rich or glamour
        attractively depraved in department store windows
    he used the large canvas, repeated portraits
        like uncut sheets of counterfeit money
    as if they were bolts of new cloth
        destined for the soul's tailor
        to cover a nakedness felt not seen
    why not replace Washington on the US dollar
        with a can of Campbell's soup?
        Andrew Jackson with gunslinger Elvis?
    how is value created by Marilyn Monroe?
        sweet Marilyn worn out and tear-stained
        but so beautiful folded in your wallet

we will never quite trust the image banks
stuff broken tokens in our mattress hearts

perhaps Andy agreed with Baudrillard after all
no value exists except value itself
but with a populist twist: in the future
we will all be wealthy for fifteen minutes

*more superficial than me, you die*
there was Andy in a TV ad
pouring paint on a personal computer
artist changed to art, eros to discos
his hard work and strict
avoidance of the articulate
his moving motion to erase himself in
with his own image
the eloquence of multiplicity
*that's not what I said*
*it's what you said*

the lonely archivist of boredom
silvery brilliant man in the moon
progressing from shy observer to
the ever-hungry, ever-observed
he leaks from his vulnerable darkness
gives birth to a love of the impossible

the wheel of fortune only seems to be spinning
since it has neither up nor down
our lovely hostess, Valerie Solanis
will show you the prizes you've won

Andy knew it was illusion
which explains why he played so well
Andy said death was too abstract for him
*they've all*, we quote him now
*gone shopping at Bloomingdale's*

## 2 / The winking nun

Leonora Carrington, living long in Mexico
rewards herself for loyal friendship
with a dreamworld
wakes in the morning with wolves
takes tea and hyena's milk for breakfast
renews her earthly life form if she chooses
as a talking iguana of speechless magic
splendid Leonora Carrington
writing the tower of dreams

her terribly wealthy English childhood
the mansion at Crookhey Hall defying art
imprisoning the debutante's landscaped heart
she made her escape just before the war
made pencil drawings of a single apple
every day for a year, while it shrivelled
and her soul grew
(look deep, no cheating)
the surrealist magnet called Paris was calling
and love, the active body, men
Max Ernst and a more rigorous training—the war
(there's your mind/body split for you)
before long Ernst was in prison and Leonora
in a Spanish lunatic asylum
grave Leonora Carrington
painting the tower of dreams

at last Mexico City, where buried dreams were always
more majestic than a sulfur sunrise
Leonora came to the home of Aztecs
an almost burnt-out case
a refugee from the tower of nightmares
she stayed suspended upside down
before the great stone door
matching gaze for gaze with serpents

her kitchen cauldron brewed mysteries
of egg temperas (Brueghel of 1942)
gorgeous eyes, hyena's eyes
moonlit hair floating on horseback
past maguey cactus, through stony
*pedregal* to visit *los Indios*

Leonora the sweetheart, the gaze of one tossed
by a century that weighs too much
one of the quizzical, sleep-deprived brides
of prisoners held by Tezcatlipoca
one of the lovers of the princes who will be sacrificed
in the propitious place of Smoking Mirror
only twenty days from now
we turn our thoughts, wife of sacrifice, to you
one who imagines she never made a decision
perceives her feminine heart purely
made of the mensal fuel of sun and moon
speak to us, art witch, of visited rituals
*The Hearing Trumpet* held before deaf ears
be a grandmother beckoning from the furthest hill

Hell is the womb of the world—or the other way 'round
crone's cauldron of exquisite death/birth
Mexico's charm lies in *las calaveras*
the skeletons drawn by Posada
*calaveras*
a cognate of tomfoolery: *la calaverada*
*y la caldera, calefacción*
some like it hot
Leonora never stood meek in the face of magic
strode moonwise through the devastated pharmacy
stole the Green Goddess's credit card
called up Taliesin, the electronic journalist
anchorman for the apocalypse
and offered wicked hints about the missing Grail

brewer of potions, reciter of spells
conjuring the end of Christianity as we know it
Leonora Carrington, weatherhawk
watching glaciers advance across the face of America
Leonora Carrington, riding and riding
the perjured white horse of identity
persuading you she never was
Leonora Carrington
who finally spews a tongue of flame
cracks masonry in the tower of dreams
emerges from the broken stump
as a huge six-winged, scaly bird
streamers of blinding light flowering
from her devil/jackal/phoenix/assassin's body
Leonora flies off...     (exit stage left and laughing)
honouring the demons in our family tree

## 3 / Yo soy la desintegración

Frida Kahlo's words:
*auxochrome* *chromophore*
colour-augmenting & colour-bearing
he the one who captured colour
she the one who gave it
he saw
she wore
Ah, Diego and Frida
Diego of the struggle, Diego of the murals
Frida of the self-portrait and the body

no one wore her body
the way Frida Kahlo did
the entire Grand Opera of Mexican life
turned to look at her
the Queen invalid
in Tehuana dress
the Aztec suffering of Catholic Mexico
her flesh, her glory
how physical pain never, ever
and yet,
*Viva Vida*, she wrote
heaven with earth forever
*de siempre*
also, *viva Diego*, *viva Stalin*
(in the cowboy ballad
where Stalin kills Trotsky
it's almost like one lover
killing the other)

such tortured histories and reckless
faith, life on a runaway streetcar
such explicit drama, stained with long blood
flowing from the Kahlo *mitológico*
so much of her was by accident

as Carlos Fuentes tells it
(can it all be true?)
a streetcar crashing into the bus she rode in 1925
breaking her spine, collarbone, ribs, pelvis
her polio-withered leg fractured in eleven places
foot crushed, left shoulder out of joint forever
and a handrail piercing her back
exiting through her vagina
parturition prohibiting children
and unbelievably, a fellow passenger and artisan
had a package of gold dust that broke open
covering her bleeding, shattered body
with shimmering gold
after such a baptism
the overstatement of high art is
simply a postcard to the folks at home:
having a legendary time
wish you could be here

Frida, in your plaster corset
like a lover severed, you pursued
your own iconic image
Frida, in your wheelchair and so often
under the salvage knife of Doctor Farill
*Alas* which means wings
grew from your broad shoulders
in the little green sketchbook of your diary
your mauve hair flies loose
and the dark, dark eyes say
I am the woman!
impassively passionate seeing
all that suffers, feeding all
with my beautiful green breasts
giving life that must die
and my body is trapped now
in this garden of prescient flames

perfume of this burning bush
the certainty flesh will not outlast it
Aren't you going?
you ask your patiently burning self
Aren't you leaving?        No.
*Alas Rotas*
broken wings

and then your death, perhaps also mythology
the cremation in an open furnace
with your friends watching
you hair burning bright like a halo
and the famous face which you made
famous by painting it so often
how it curled then
into a farewell smile
*espero alegre la salida*
*y espero no volver jamás*

pray for us, Santa Frida
patroness of unnoticed, unpraised art
intercede for us
in the vast eye of the universe

## 4 / Rhyging in Babylon

a globalization take on
        Robert Nesta Marley
deprivation, eventual beatification and
        Bob

go trash the easy biographies
        that make everybody feel okay
and the flacks who tell us how the ghetto boys
        succeeded by doing it their own way
you can't separate the Wailers' cry
        from the buffalo soldier rides again
your Euro-plural, multicultural
        lies have not put oppression to an end

            get up, stand up
    Nesta, where ya gone dis yere day?
            get up, stand up
    music mustn't work for no CIA

all through the student ghetto
        funky bedrooms of the future elite
I see posters of Bob Marley
        smoking a spliff to the reggae beat
sanitized rebellion, child
        you drop your beer bottles in the grass
but six o'clock the next morning
        you never seem to notice when the bottle-pickers pass

            get up, stand up
    stand with the rest of us
            open up your eyes
        how many rivers do we have to cross
        before we can learn how to talk like the boss

fleeting unity, birth of hypocrisy, for one moment
        every person was a free citizen

in the empire of runaway slaves
Bob Marley decreed there would be
no passports and no borders
even the leaders of political nations
were crowing the rhetoric of liberation
at the crowded demonstration

but never trust the rival empire
when your under-capitalized back is turned
the Marley legend is caught and re-coded
as the happy effect of international trade
and white bankers, smiling obeahmen of the North
who practice money magic in secret
have turned third world populations
into duppy slaves

World Pirates and IMF rob I
sold I to the merchant ships
promise to pull our economy
from the bottomless pit

and the mystic G-7, council of the wise
will direct the world economy with pure impartiality
they have generous hearts, they have fat wallets
as leaders of the new world order
they ask nothing for themselves
just a few cheap mangoes, cheap bauxite
only a few more songs

how long shall they keep our profits
while we stand aside and look
some say it's just a part of it
we've got to balance the books

won't you help to sing
get up, stand up
because all that I've ever had

is burning tonight
in the fever of redemption songs
we hoped would inoculate us
against the great disease
which even now is raging
from Trenchtown to Toronto
collapsing the fractured, sodden house
of your ancient social architecture

the future always arrives too late
and what do we replace it with?
the exodus from funky Babylon
has been postponed until the next eternity arrives
sweet freedom, dignity and loyalty
the fantasy of post-liberal democracy
*we ran ting, ting no ran we*
are you satisfied
with the life you're living?

## 5 / Prothalamium for Allen G.

and when he came
        all the mute birds sang
when he came with his mouth
        white breath and Tantric energy
when he came and came and loosened his throat
        to receive the white hot expansion torrent
        of deep breath a movement from the chest
        his white breath fluttered and whispered
        with a Paterson accent
        inhaled again before chanting down
        on the next, long, fat stanza
and all the deaf animals listened intensely
        all the sunflowers burst into psalms
        tiny animals floated through the airline cabin
        and skyscrapers wiggled their stone hips

*Hare* bare-naked circumference of the Allen Ginsberg dream
        foolscap, ruled and spiral note worlds that
        still extrude glossy thought balloons of scandal
        irresistible words to the evil nemesis Censor
        who longs to have you black-taped as porn

thought balloons that are popping ever since you left us
        being licked by the vulgar, gum-cracking tongues
        that juice us, jizz us, make us wild
        imitators stung, swinging with the buzz
        of espresso bees in the bonnet of philosophy
we hear your rhythm, we have become
        your second, not-so-best thought, you might say
oh Allen, we want instant enlightenment
        without the study that comes before

shapely thought, shapely mind, shapely shapely
        more than inspiration's slap
        Hark! The thighs Hark!
        To thy comely dick

Harken to the assholes, hark!
in ever-stricter times the mechanical rhythm looms
despite the inner will to listen
and defeat fear, more specifically revulsion
despite the gentle win on cruise control
a stricter time pounded with rhythm sticks
pricks that kick and the paranoia norm
reactionary really, the way you'd expect
—drugs in the public washroom
desire everywhere you turn
seldom celebrated, just used
doomed and disposed of

while you were alive, you left a message
catching self in journals
photographing in mirrors, mirrors
receding, Moscow Manhattan Colorado
while you were alive, transmitted electrically
kissed the one flower that said
others would come, keep trying
so you spoke, so you breathed
'cause you knew others would come
so you moved closer, talked all night
sweet hairy wag-dick Allen
Allen beyond us now but here beyond
because the poem resides in the head
because the poem looks good in a suit
because the poem will at last be comfortable
in Pearl River, Bangor Maine, or Smiths Falls Ontario
you just said and kept on saying
keep it simple, wear erudition lightly
how rounded you were, how shining
strung out on human love

a poet's career of public appetite and compulsory quests
for lovers and the sometimes desperate access

to an always acceptably mystical cool
a sensual route to a shriven soul
don't worry about the guru's rod anymore
poets are forgiven, poets are
wedded to eternity when they die
poets get to choose
the best man on their wedding night

## 6 / Mixed at Scream / Mixed at Bad Animals

(an imaginary dialogue for Kurt Cobain and Courtney Love)

*it's okay to eat fish 'cause they don't have any feelings*
–Kurt Cobain, "Something In The Way"

*KC:*
*here we are now—spitting like a tree'd lynx*
*reeking with chronic depression's humid heat*

CL:
sleep with me, wake up alive
vivid through this transition jive

*a generation of vipers on guitar*
provoke the bitching spirit walking
*shocked through the head with what*
it keeps us achingly, wakingly here
*still doesn't give me satisfaction*
bring on the green witch mean times of life
*here we are now—blessed with genuine bones*
oh life
*and the smoke ring of flesh incense*
oh life of lying
*fried nuclear kids puzzling over the cult*
—oh man
*of alien personality, the deification of empathy*
sometimes everything
*the impish possibility of healers*
you do
*we walk the railroad tracks of industrial decay*
makes me sick
*rites of passage under the bridge*
*slurring the fucking sacred chant*
just go ahead and try to turn off
*that might bring home a prodigal god*
passion superheated
*we are ejecting the warp core of lost humanity*

try to shut me up
*jesus*
try to turn away
*someone help us in this*
I know your slow degradation, dickhead
*din of inequity*

I stripped naked for what I believed
*but I'm corrosion, the stomach's acid bath*
and even if you just believe in not believing
just believe in who gives a fuck
*and I'm never coming back this time*
don't walk away
*even if your body is a fucking shrine*
don't succumb
*prayers out of the prions of love*
to that better-to-burn-out shit
*Love the name you elected*
remember I'm your flame
*Love endowed by your deadhead father*
*can't even speak of Courtney unless*
*we say the word —love*
fuck off
*up yours*
dick drip
*you think this is holy or whatever*
thought I was a fucking match for you
*but how the fuck should I know*
my better-burn-than-fade lover
*I like who you fucking are*
I thought you were so hot
*but I'm gone*
what about Frances?
*never coming back*
and what about rock and roll?
*spa cure, long weekend*

what about me, you asshole?
*take the rest of your life off*
what about Frances?
*get 'way from me, go down with me*
what about rock and roll?
*it won't make any indifference*
what about me, you asshole?
*there we were now*
what about Frances?
*there I never quite was*
what about rock and roll?
*don't care if anyone calls it a ploy*
what about me, you asshole?
*stupid posturing of the damned*
I made our bed
*borne happy under the chilly toadstool*
I'll lie in it
*of function/dysfunction/dis/Dis*
I made our bed
*funk machinery death*
had our child in it
*I mean no big deal*
any idea how that feels?
*just the ordinary torment*
wanna talk to me about sad pissing empathy?

*put saliva mouth on the television plug*
poor hungry death
*slice the hand that bleeds*
starving for another rock star
*stick your monkey in the jar*
poor midnight snack
*do you know what I'm saying?*
death must have been desperate
*how power comes from both*
so no more promises

no more die for you bullshit
*love and the barrel of a gun*
no more kill the family save the son
*c'mere go'way c'mere*
only save the daughter this time
*go'way c'mere go'way*
I will tell Frances she is loved
*c'mere go'way c'mere*
saying it over and over
*go'way you lovesick cunt*
love like a name
*shake the dead snake rattle*
whispered when we're sleeping
*I'm gettin out of town tonight*
say it to me
*I swear I've given my guns away*
just once
*no I don't have a gun*
say it to me
*I swear*
just once
*I don't have a gun*
say it to me
*I don't have a gun*
just once
*I don't have a gun*

## 7 / The flight of Walter Benjamin

weary traveller, wandering sage
        what brings you to this hotel in Port-Bou?
            there are no exit visas here

plump voyager, stateless Jew, child of Berlin
        the ship that could take you to New York
            exists beyond the veil of night, in Messianic time
        and you lie trapped in a seedy Spanish room
            sleepless between historical-materialist sheets

Walter Benjamin, elusive thinker, critic of everyone
        the hotel owner is a fascist sympathizer
            even now phoning the town police
        to have you and all the refugees escorted
            through the mountains you just crossed
        on goat tracks that make old hearts split open
            over the French border where the guards
        deliver foreigners to the boxcars of the Germans

no one can escape the aesthetics of war
        unless you were thinking perhaps
            of the morphine tablets
            in the lining of your coat

in your final notes on the philosophy of history
        you chose Paul Klee's angel
            a favourite drawing you owned
        the little Angelus Novus composed
            of tendril lines like ivy, you made
            him the astonished angel of History
        but more than you could know
            you were writing of yourself

the Kingdom of Truth always immanent for you
            the right thought could any moment clear error
        so Angelus Novus arrives in his chariot

an armoured tank drawn by dogs and eagles
he fetches you the way gods send for prophets
fires in the sky, trumpets made of bone
because you, Walter, are the real Angel of History
and History craves disaster, as you must know
from Carthage to the Reichstag the only
clear limit to human power and atrocity
is temporal, not sacred
time itself gets fed up and prompts
new tyrants to remove the old

it is perdition, is it not?
flying backwards like this
eyes open, seeing clearly
in one painful, timeless glance
the poets, scholars, warriors, and kings
civilization's long, wrong advance
to see the mushroom clouds and cities
the gas chambers and arcades
the insight must be painfully clear

and while you cling tenderly to brave Angelus Novus
wreckage on wreckage
piling at your feet
a great wind from Paradise is eternally pulling
yanking the chariot, turning metal
tank treads faster than cinema reels
toward a future that never ends, never lasts
you are leaving now and the angel
gently discards your embrace
allows you to recede, a sentinel alone
amid the storm called progress

## 8 / *The quest of the little folk*
*(with thanks and a tip of the hat to Ian MacKay)*

how cruel to be critical about Maud Lewis
        celebrated garden gnome of Nova Scotian heritage
how rude to stick your tongue out
        at cruelty memorialized, heritage of the disinherited
the museums have worked so hard to preserve
        Maud's home, her decorated and muralled
        deathly poor shack by the road
and the purveyors and publishers of tourist culture
        have brought out the art books
        the greeting cards, the tour

yet one can't help thinking about her paintings for sale
        like vegetables by the roadside
            or farm fresh eggs
        dirt cheap, a great deal
            and you were helping the poor
her images appreciating in value
        a bull market with bells on, as Nova Scotia froze
        in the oncoming headlights of the notion of folk
and the magazines in Ontario gushed
        "Frail Woman With A Bold Brush"
            yet no plumbing, no electricity
        just a dangerous woodstove
            that Everett scrounged from a neighbour's barn

perhaps there's no charity in lovers of art
        customers only, glad for a bargain
        aesthetic pleasure at rock-bottom prices
but why proclaim her to be well-loved
            once she was dead?
we love the media image of simple, happy folk
        Maud and Ev as shoemaker's elves
        making secret paintings overnight
and the paintings themselves, bright happy wishes

for a safe Yarmouth girlhood she didn't have
raised by her brother after their parents died
then a secret baby, a quick adoption
and the brother sent her away

the paintings in uncluttered primary colours
not documents of nostalgia or deep roots
but exile, bitterness barely forgiven
and the inflated price sometimes paid
for escaping one life and choosing another
a minimal life that she must have cherished
arthritic, crippled Maud
inhaling paint fumes by the stove
somehow doing the work she loved
while Everett, country miser
sold fish door to door
and the people who pulled up in their cars
to look at Maud's paintings must have said:
gosh, such simple folks, they wouldn't know
what to do with money, even if they had it

picture Maud in the evening
hands cramped, shoulders sore
and Everett leaning through lamplight to touch her
who knows how, or what he said
their bodies and unspoken feelings gone
to legends for the curious, but quite as real
and enigmatic as anyone's skin, marked
with soot from mortality's lantern

this is our heritage:
every summer we commence to singin'
them ole tourist industry blues
oh, I wuz so poe-ah once
maa-yaan, I had to make Art
we sing the song often, familiar with the tune

guitar case open on the sidewalk
portable coffin filling with coins
we use irony, but believe me it isn't
appropriation exactly
more like the wild roses
of truly creating have no place
and Maud's bottomless poverty, ripped from her life
endures as image, an artefact
made humble and safe to consume

## 9 / The heart not as a symbol

lying on a couch in a borrowed sleeping bag
listening to the wind outside of what passes
for a living room in Dale Williams's apartment
the student ghetto, 1976
snow gets shoved down Brock Street, Kingston
brusque and blinding under amber streetlights
conversations are ended, traffic halted
no one's going home tonight

young Dale with raggedy beard and glasses, frail but wild
a farm family background outside of Cornwall, Ont
father that never figured out
why Dale wrote poetry
and was a scrawny, breathless bookworm
with congenital heart defects
why Dale couldn't be a dairy farmer
a pigeon chest too familiar with the surgeon's knife

Dale wrote a column for Alive magazine
the newsprint temple to vicious infighting
among jittery Ontario Maoists
and there beside paeans to Enver Hoxha
were Dale's homespun essays, meditations on rural folklore
under his pen name: The Maple Street Collector
he gathered sayings, expressions, the proverbs of mockery
in subtle undercurrents of resistance
—Can't the cat look at the Queen?
I hear the wind and the silence
Dale must be sleeping in his turmoiled room
no one can go home tonight

we traded poems, green ideas, impressions
the first real writing in our lives
his poems coming from a blood-soaked place
where he dissected doctors
and remembered sad, distant hospitals

open heart poems of operations, the tortured
body becoming pale extension of procedure
in our dialogue, I played the immigrant
a puzzled interloper from New England
not yet at home in the Limestone City
but Dale was displaced, too, in his role
a son-of-the-soil weakling, unfit observer
wan lover of a community
that valued work, drink, and loyalty
in that rough masculine order
what could they do with a runt?
—let him write

Dale, an exile from the land of wellness
perceived the misperceptions, the distance
how we would grieve and love belatedly
he knew the temporarily-abled lacked nerve
in his true north differently strong and free
and he snagged rough snapshots in his novice poems

that spring he decided to go to Boston
Mass General had a new set of techniques
that might be worth trying
Dale gambled on the idea of healing
because he'd been told he would die young
wrote letters and poems during convalescence
went home to his father's place, still recovering
until one kitchen night
he arched his back, convulsed in the wooden chair
died within minutes

his poems are lost as far as I know
the family saw no point
but I think of lying on a couch with spilt innards
and wonder at Dale's courage
worry that I can't hear his breathing

hope he's all right
in weather so deep, so unforgiving
undamaged, we stay put on lumpy cushions
nurse our feelings, wait for sunrise
no one can go home tonight

## 10 / Franz Berwald

*i.*

your life did not lack beauty, old composer
when symphonies unfurled in your head
creative-workaholic, inkpot at the piano
in an age before wireless and phonograph
before Sweden had professional orchestras
when musical thoughts stayed mainly thoughts
a gifted Swedish child of German parents
you embraced music, held on tight
dreamed the elsewhere of high culture
if you couldn't slake passions in the slant Nordic light
the no-applause of no-audience at dusk
you would go to Europe where there waited
glory and glitter for the price of a song

Vienna in 1842 was the sweetest
Jenny Lind sang your work and success
improved every cake, every sip of wine
compositions flowed like the Danube
they loved you all season long
Berlin, then Paris—more training, more recognition
finally, why not go home to Sweden?
your career well established and surely
Stockholm would drown in delirious cheers

overland by coach on long, muddy roads
to Lübeck through dangerous forests
and across the stormy Baltic to home
to find that praise didn't travel well, and your lustre
was dimmed by salt water passage
the old neighbours had your number

*ii.*

back then the cobblestones in Gustav Adolf Square
were synonymous with progress
a brace of foreign ships in the harbour
the commerce of onward and upward
the critics figured Berwald was pretty good
but too much like Beethoven, not enough Mozart
too emotional and inflected with Teutonic darkness
orchestral music should never plunge and veer
this way, violently submitting
to the sacred force that would shred it
contemporary taste said wear your inspiration
with reserve, lightly
composers must be sober
Franz, what did you expect from the critics
who complained that the Ode to Joy
sounded like a pack of shrieking
Tierra del Fuegans fighting over raw fish?

*iii.*

blessed with business-sense, Berwald
changed course and became the manager
of Sandö glassworks at Norrland
1850 to '58
even part-owner by the end
if Berwald could have met Wallace Stevens
or shared a railroad carriage with Charles Ives
he'd have recognized his heirs
descendants of the modern compromise
money versus art, they knew wasn't
a huge problem—just get the money

under loitering October clouds, retirement in a country home
a veil of woodsmoke suspended among pearly aspens
the grove of smooth half-lit skin
slender trunks corseted in dim light

old Berwald composed again, saving his notes
redeeming the secret Northern life
playing arrangements with his daughter
theirs the scherzo of the flower folded
inside the adagio of economic living
making peace with obscurity

*Coda.*
much changed, twentieth-century Sweden
meant paved roads, state radio
a modern culture, a different building
to house the latest idea of a nation
Berwald's forgotten music, but preserved
by his daughter, had the right touch
of Beethovian grandeur—it sounded
like a modern part of a greater Europe
true, a Sibelius or a Grieg would have been better
than sour old Franz scowling in a stiff collar
looking annoyed at his late recognition
posthumous gold watch and handshake
just like Canada, we want heroes to smile
and notice that we remember now

don't depend on history, a frowning Berwald seems to say
the weak, pretty flame some call applause
the grateful nations, the flickering shadows
look rather for the rare and subtle sound
a wind shaking the clump of hawthorns
the piano's last, vibrating chord
listen to the curious glowing dreams
that crowd about your window
old stories half-sung around fading fires
about trolls and fairies and strange music
that leads, if we are lucky and strong enough
deeper, ever deeper into the forest

## II / We *want* to be Patti Smith

something about a rocker/poet/seeker
something about Tarkovsky and the allotted function of art
    which is not to serve us, not to fuck with ideas
        but to prepare us for death
    plough our souls and thrash our bodies to make us
        a possible receptacle of His will
        make us capable of something
about the widow of death, bride of pain
    her life in red and black fleshtones
        hair still long, only now going gray

about us long-haired, fashion-conscious poets
        with our undreamt dreams and virgin wrists
    longing to be the icons we are not, we are not
        weeping and tasting the ocean, we are not
        choking on our own vomit while thinking of loss
    and we are not dedicating our lives
            to Him, unnamed
            because he is more precious
            and higher than we

we want the time to be now
    we want the children to be ours
        we want to live Patti Smith's life
we want Robert Mapplethorpe to be our roommate
    with drugs, photography, endless spiralling night
        —he will never clean the bathroom once
        yet he'll bitch about the state of the kitchen
we want to quit our own legends and move to Motor City with
                                                                                    Frederick
    have our children and only play guitar
        on anniversaries and other lonely nights
    to remind ourselves of the way we traded
        the loneliness of prophecy
        for the loneliness of motherhood

that ultimate in destructive self-abandon
giving our blood in the form of other lives
torn from our bodies, then torn from our hands

we want to be Patti Smith
and we want to bay like hounds in pursuit of love
want to claw at the insides of our glass bodies
punch holes in the screwed-down lid of the sky
steal wafers of tragedy from the paupers' breakfast
and that is why we skinny long-haired poseurs
rock and roll niggers, space monkeys
have to cast off the white snakeskin of society
why we bleed unscrupulously in the gutter

we want to be Patti Smith
and emerge from passion's opium pipe
spraying sweat and spit and secretions
be furies of the millennium, hypnotic fiery beings
guaranteed to give everybody a hard-on
that lasts well into the next century
we want to be sirens and the Greek mast and the traveller
and we will lash ourselves to the music of desire
transcending the jagged rocks
which also stand for us, teeth of victory
broken flags of despair
waving

**hey you**
**get up**

we rock
and roll down here with the waves
that is why we are an aria of flesh
and why the planet crumbles around us
as we demand entrance
into heaven

## 12 / Ain't no more in this world
(a lament for Jimi Hendrix)

oh Jimmy James & the Blue Flames
    oh enigma frozen at the age of 27
    rainbow
        bridges
        freeze before roads
    and with you I see a traffic jam
        straight up ahead

oh baby sorcerer, dionysius awake
    your waa-waa and your wailing guitar
        your 3am feeding, oh baby
        what was in your stomach
            half-digested rice
            —and when did you eat it?
        more wine in your stomach than your bloodstream
            —when did you drink it?
        wine wine wine, hey sugar
            pass that bottle to me
        and where the hell are those sleeping pills?

you were standing next to a mountain
        gonna break your hand
        tryin to chop it down
    a message to love, a semaphore
        signal-to-noise ratio
        freedom, freedom
    feel like I'm living at the bottom of a grave
        peace, happiness and all that other bullshit

picture your last concert Jimi
    —did you see it all beforehand?
        cold island on the Baltic Sea
        fucking Gotterdämmerung storm pounding the stage
        German bikers yelling racist insults
                *Go Home!*

ain't got no home on this world

oh jumpin Jimi
ex-boy scout, ex-paratrooper
magnet for pain and pleasure
let me stand next to your friendly fire

nine Vesparax, Jimi
continental barbituates
18 times the normal dose, babe
more than enough to inhibit the body's
reflexes, more than
too much
that stomach full of wine became
a lung full which poured out
as the doctors tried to revive you
you drowned

and all that time you sang about
a man who could live and breathe underwater
about people going elsewhere
did you want the party to end?
were you sick of it?
did you just make a mistake?
manic depression
ain't no life no where
is this love or confusion?
is it tomorrow
or just the end of time?

excuse me, Jimi
gotta go, babe
gotta kiss the sky goodbye

## 13 / The middle finger of his right hand

the transformation on stage, moving deeper
inside any given eternal moment
seat-of-the-pants shamanism
everything else was details

somebody's jugband, some Bay baby's guitarman
the roots of rock and roll, ripped
tripped on Hashbury's communal joint
Jerry Garcia, about those first days
were they really the hardest days?
or the later ones, the recycling years
with more than a touch of gray
like the morning sun you came
and like the wind you didn't mean goodbye
you meant more mileage, please
from this great big American car

this perfect rose, this perfect road
a cigarette and a cup of coffee
a skeletal search for natural wisdom
and my body is an overloaded bus in the ditch
6,000 pounds of gear
one final tour

the father who didn't grow up
the Buddha with no particular message
the man who didn't dominate the rap, Jack
beat the day he watched his Daddy die
beat and hip and honked on the white stuff
wired to the big amp
come, hear Uncle Sam's band
by the riverside, got some demons to lay to rest
here beside the tie-dyed
this darkness has got to give and give
till it just gives out

in flavour-of-the-month country
Cherry Garcia had legs
the appeal of an honest man with no answers
the perfection of no pretension
and almost satori
on the nomadic party-time concert tour
Captain Trips and stumbles
just like the rest of us
he shelters in the chemical quest for awhile
till his final drying days
and a last lurch for sobriety
pitches him from the moving train
a workingman's death

not a word of advice, bless his bones
for forbearance and the long solos
so low and so long
to step out of the spotlight

you were having a hard time
living the good life

## 14 / Bugsy Burns

d'ye ken my auld friend Robbie
talkin to a louse?
he never larned a trade
he never done a day's work
in his life, and the lad must be daft
to sit there talkin to a bug
then go home and write
a poem about it

I'll bet if you were him
you might have told the lady
in some polite way
or killed the little bloodsucker
or minded your own business
ignored the beast for decency's sake
not strike up a conversation with it
but Robbie chatters on and on
that's the way he is, the little sot
until he slams into the last stanza
and leaves a scar on the world:
*to see ourselves as others see us*

how can the line survive so long
entering the language like a spliced gene?
how is it that long after the whiskey
has been pissed away, and long after
the lady and the louse have died
after the bottles have been broken and crushed
into powdery dust that washes off the street
it still says the right thing?

might it not be worth ten PhDs
in entomology, gained by sleeping
with the dirtiest drunks you could find
night after night, picking nits
from their long, filthy hair

if you could be given one perfect line
just like that

your life for a split second would be beyond
the starvation of anger, the greed
life would grant you the good sleep
of a deeply beloved child
but your need would come back
finding you where you'd lost it
crowding your happiness
more cigarettes, more possessions, more jobs
new reasons to sell odd pieces of your life
doctor's appointments and expensive prescriptions
possibly an operation

Robbie, old rain father, if once we had
such a moment, our starving needs
would crush into perfect stillness
anything resembling
a clear statement, a blue sky

so let me sing blank verses, and mix whiskey with mud
let us close our heads and empty our black hearts
dismissing the warm wishes of the moment because
we might fall on our goddamn knees...   breaking down
the lacunae of intentions and poems   we
might   pierce
words we can't enter
then...
what other vessel will catch us
as we trip o'er the curb
what other eyes reflect back
steer us home tonight
nodding with recognition to   this brooding syntax

Icon ?
gimme your keys you shouldn't be drivin'...
o'er the brink
hiccup

## 15 / *Photographer with labyrinth*

semi-anonymous photographer
his selection process, into and falling
out of narrative heaven
is neither completely unconscious of the nude
nor a static suggestion of what might
the clothing dropped
act outside the frame
towards completion
always, the pornographer whispers always
pure joy just beyond the confines
of this light-stopped space

prides himself on professionalism
making the girls comfortable and seizing
the moment—intuition, the individual shot
he seems close to no volition
ecstatic as crowded psychology
in the walk/don't walk zones of fashion
but he's mumbling temptation's mantra
sounds like Catullus praying:
dismember some other man
chthonic hurricane, not me

the photographer makes choices, which model
what lighting, and then goes
deep inside the moment's work, just moving
not knowing what she really gives up until
he does the contact sheet
but this one, warrior goddess, is truly present
she looks like lightning in a jar
or something Bacchic striking through
in the darkroom of his skull, he begins to stumble
over contradictions, con-
tractions of male gaze

full body contact proofs
a touch of vast action, slice of real
each looking tonight is active, filled with fantasies
pre-wish across the aesthetic skin, sheer dream
brave something else, he dares to think
projected spirit in unmobility
goddesshood, lip glossolalia
slippery otherness around the corner
more powerful, turns the maze
into gaze she returns forever

he is minotaur—horns of metal, lens eyes
electronic flash
and she is the subject armed
hungry mother with naked sword
whenever he waves his camera at her
giving the orders, he startles himself
starts to feel
his lower half, the trembling manbody
will be separated from his head
he is vulnerable to this girl
who knows her way home
grasps the thread

he loads more film
gets off a shot, but she skewers
him in the f-stop
of his trapped watching
snared behind the shutter
by what little softness dwelt in the eyes

gaze that now hardens fast
prolonging desperation
he retreats ever further in his darkroom
senses somehow he's been gored
he ponders lenses and, craftsmanlike

sets the timer, waits for prints
waits for something to develop

and now he's breathing strangely, plainly staring
at the magic empty baths in the dimming red glow
there are no pictures, just dark trays
that slowly fill with his blood

## 16 / *Disaster as a value*

welcome back to the tower of dreams
pilgrim
all the time while you were gone
the shattered masonry clattered on
and pulverized slow-motion falling
stones blossomed in the air
blessèd rebel thunder

when you were here last
the Dalai Lama was young
Elvis was joining the US Army
and those beautiful sea-green
Chevrolet Impalas with black
convertible tops and white sidewalls
were rolling off assembly lines
down freshly paved roads
bursting through guardrails
and flipping down embankments
brief airborne examples
of modern form over function
this was 1959
Elvis joked shyly with the press
Sartre mused on the existential
and Chinese troops were approaching Lhasa
surrounding the Buddhist monasteries of Tibet
once the largest universities in the world
the People's Liberation Army
turning traditions older than Oxford
into lost mandalas of coloured sand
dispersed in the rivers of History

and from her lonely walls around the palace at Troy
Helen looked out and saw the ocean of wisdom
aum mani pad-me hum
perceived fire darting from the god's and goddess's hands

causing towers to flower and the boats on Aegean beaches
to burn like cradles
whose ashes are seeds
that the birds will carry
far beyond mountains
to the great cities of the plain
where the people lack for nothing
and their values are respected
while their souls weep

Shangri-la/Shambhala, Tibet
over decades our symbol
of a distant, perfect holiness
one that our greed, our eyes and hands
and the Midas touch of history
could only ruin on contact
the China of Mao was an abused, colonial child
our best student, inheritor of sorrow
and dialectical materialism
when I choose to weigh my possessions
against yours—who is exploited?
which is the oppressor?
the dark demons of materialism
sing in loud voices
you've paved paradise
and put up a prison camp

in ancient times, before the great monasteries
Lopon Rinpoche was asked by the faithful
to come and tame the many demons of Tibet
yet he drank for many days in a Tibetan tavern
until the furious owner demanded payment
—be patient, he told her, I'll pay at sundown
then he pulled out his *phurbu*, mystic dagger
drove it through the shaft of sunlight in the doorway
making the sun stop for three more days

—release the sun, pleaded the farmers and herdsmen
—first give me alms, that I might pay the innkeeper
in great awe the villagers paid, the sun was allowed to set
and the innkeeper became Lopon's disciple

oh jewel in the lotus, pollen on the winds
of protest from Dharamsala to London
a red-robed monk holds up a
sign
with cartoon soldiers beating a monk
and lettered words:
*PEACE HAS NO VALUE*
which could be an end
of the world statement
denial of equivalence
bad English, or knowledge
that value dies
all equations will be broken

and now Buddhism becomes North American
a peaceful, achievement-oriented discipline
for the elite in the hills above LA
middle-class boomers in the south end of Halifax
mail-order devotional aids, plus shipping
and we can believe whatever we want
to believe, yet we really
want the radical eruption
even or beyond meaning
the singularity absolute, illumination
carried with only minor destruction
to the pulsing heart of the world

## 17 / Poem without a heroine

this is what it means to be a poet
Jack Spicer, Anne Sexton, Anna Akhmatova
to roll the great stone around the city square
but where Spicer would remove
the personal from the poem
Akhmatova waits for History
to enter her room
*They took you away at the break of dawn,*
*and in so doing, they sentenced us both.*
*Down the corridor the children were crying,*
*near the icon-shelf the holy candle choked.*
*Your lips were cold from the icon's kiss.*
*And the sweat of death on your body—I'll never forget.*
*Today, like the wife of a captured mutineer,*
*I can only stand below the Kremlin's turrets and howl.*

so you wanna be a cultural star
but look, darling, not everyone is
the stars are never chosen at random
think about Akhmatova in 1913, the Stray Dog Café in Petrograd
how she, the gorgeous poet, made every head
turn, every mouth exclaim, Akhmatova
and how she took no solace from this
only played her part in some obscure drama
produced by magnetic folds in the mantle of a prophet
who has the blues way down in her soul
knows a raw sadness before it happens
knows too, she will pay for this
(the envelope, please... )

the revolution came—and scorn, isolation
her ex-husband shot for supposed treason
and the men she turned to for protection
became jealous, confined her, burned her poems
meanwhile the Writers' Union, firmly the Party's instrument

called her work obsolete, and her
anathema, an enemy of the people's glory
when the police took her son to prison
it was for being the son of Akhmatova

*Requiem*
had to be copied in secret on cigarette papers
recited then burnt after being learned by heart
the poems which survived became untarnished prayers
the untainted wells of Russian confession
told over and over like rosaries
her words discovered how to procreate in the dark
her themes were the memes of compassion
remembrance outliving the reign of terror

Stella Maris, through blitzkriegs and betrayal
an ocean spills from your every breast
one love quenches, one blood arrests
Stalin's boot heels and the wheels of the black maria
the state tries to decide if suffering is allowed in public
but the secret communion of the purges
the corpse-laden siege of Leningrad
will eventually unite women of all classes

Akhmatova, inspiration for a new generation in the Sixties
a voice outside the prison gates of 1937
how the remarkable was drawn to you, our star
our dark seer, recording eye
celebrity and notoriety preceding you
was History just the unhappy family
you were born to? the family
that hadn't meant any harm
but ruined our lives nonetheless? —not likely
something that a star does inside poems
something about a point of light like you
renders language unforgivable

the vain brutality of dictators and bad poets
        is inflamed by the star's performance
the greater the darkness of night, the more
        you absorbed our gaze, Akhmatova
the more tragedy, the more there was to metabolize
        just as willows bathe at rivers
        absorbing light and the corpses
        that descend into ground

Stella Maris, who were you?
    the woman I perpetually miss?
    the light of thoughts that once played across my skin?
    the one I may not know?
    my mother was much too young, breastless and dying
    the brittle darkness yet carries us all
            to and from
on certain nights death barely pauses here
        offers no one kisses good-bye
    our Sylvia snuffs out the pilot light
        Marilyn cries one last time on her pillow
    Mayakovsky and all the twinkling stars
            cast down their lances

what does it mean to be a poet?
        Jack Spicer, Anne Sexton
        Anna Akhmatova

and learned to live as you and I
longed to: a poet/derelict/free spirit
alcoholic in the mirror looking back
move your telephone to the dining room table
have another cigar, don't let up
you've got at least another week to live
in the famous alley of ashcans
with dustbin bohemians and worn
lyrical anarchists, vegetarian dopers
our notebooks, journals meticulously
collected over five years then thrown
like angel wings from a subway platform

we write crude verses, oh dwelling of Horus
and if our pressed and dried sentiments
should ever reach you, remember:
Daniel Jones, Shaunt Basmajian, Robert Billings
all of us
wanted to be writers
somewhere to go, something to do
buried deep in delusions
to be writers recording these times
transcending what we never desired
writers with unique and terrible visions
of the wheel that isn't round
the damaged fire burning hot
hitting the terrifying flight paths
of metal fatigue and the oldest world
only to pour wind on the sounds
spill words on the end of everything
words themselves to be destroyed
life force forgotten in the brain-scan linguistic
Western hemorrhage of Sappho's fragments

Gwendolyn MacEwen, you are and were the model
        and skies are the milky limit of human kindness
        print information magic summoned binds
        the dream-state executors together
a distrust of the real slips through our fingers
        invisible guilt pounding like neutrons
            at the bottom of a Sudbury mineshaft
        every poem a shattering, dissolving
            the very tiny notion of a self

thus half a generation later
        one scruffy young prince goes questing
        riding the Danforth subway on splendid white sneakers
    carrying a sword, a wilted lily
        he kneels on the steps of 13 Browning Ave
        and waits for the goddess to bare
        her beautiful negative radiance
    oh the horizon of enormous gravity
        the imprint of the telephone on her abdomen

can't take it with you, the prince knows
        can't say you can't take it
    he wishes he could relocate trace elements
        of courage in the isolation
        of the invisible apartment afterworld
            isotopes of love

in his vision that night he sees Hathor
        and tries to look up her skirt
        as she ascends the escalator to eternity
when she reaches the top, she is
        elemental, a type of absence
        pure catalyst in the ferment of heaven

## 19 / Sunship

John Coltrane is still searching for the mystery modal node
the aural version of god's word
divine intervals
though breath no longer flows in and out through the flesh
bold container of his body and that thing
that thing you know blowing crazy with the spirit outside
of parallel solar wind lines differential dreaming
tangled in the sheets of sound and the downpour lost
arpeggios like a jazz Milarepa in a stomach cavern
Hey demons, I know you demons
that moan in the back doors of time
I am not so
I am not so
I am African
and not so afraid

ah our aid, oh Love
it all has to do with it
my Lord is necessary soundtrack to the big bang in Alabama
creation, ideeeation, eeeelation
elegance
exaltation
fit it all in and then—take the solo, Kokopelli
though some said Trane was wrecking
western harmony
Europiano musical values
in his quest for the sun/the sound/*le son*
miss universe dust disquieting lyric interface with a minor
chord it, cover it, tear it, mode it, wear it, swallow it, blow it
it looks good on you
you're welcome
we will vote for the mystic of our choice
this is america
*he will remake us... he always has and he always will*
thank you god

you're welcome
there may be peace and love and perfection
using every chance at creation
oh lord
welcome

to that sweet baby on horseback, to that embouchure
don't you just love the word
welcome to the naked king
embouchure under Sol's rays, hot bell enflammée
Coltrane's joy was euphoric and warm
his ferocious trust
a sun's energy, a type of giving
remote and the sun doesn't give a damn
it's the feeling that counts
skin burnt and the heartless hepatoma
same drought levels all
plays all twelve notes on the solo
teeth gone
anyway
so what for spacious skies
and the photons and pleasures mixed with bad junk
poured into a vial too small
radio breaking what it sustains, what it sings
a very dangerous card
on Monday the lunatics are not mad
but the sunstruck are
Vincent van Gogh and all the monks
Thelonius and Merton and Thoreau
maybe a true sun says that it's not the sun
just looking thank you Lord
but in the background, fusty Glenn Gould hums
and
old Swinburne sways
gets to his feet
begins to jump up and down on his bed declaiming

pumping pre-Raphaelite verse at the top of his voice
which is
merely a trick to make you leave the door ajar again
whereupon he takes to his heels
down the alley to the village vanguard
with you pursuing madly
polyrhythmic footsteps in the hallway
let the vinyl records show
cousin Elvis dancing in the syncretism of the sun
the sunglasses of Jackie O
perched on a white kerchief let it show
certain planets hanging forever above the gravity well
of extremely gratifying solos

oh tonic chorus of welcome
shamans and gentlemen, to the last set of the evening
may we know the true sun by our wisdom
that knowledge is nothing like the sun
or the stars, or the whole thing
no one ever is
no one ever falls without the ballads
no failings without the rain
sublime ingenuity of the Lord
and whatever passes
for a love supreme
our tender heartfires roaring
on tenor sound
Coltrane's tone
offering
what magic

passes

on

## 20 / Zizanie

*(to the memory of Karen Zalubas, Reading, Massachusetts)*

imperfectly imagined, my inner life
    is a wicked forest of few paths
        and those well-worn and circular
a summer world, incomplete yet ending
    just beyond the skin of my fingers
        unfelt, unvirused, out of reach
true, sometimes I see and hear
        but references alone
    your feminine body reflective
        the unamusement park of our love
            the miseryhouse mirrors

I tried once to see outside of my life
    and saw only the back of my head
        curvature of space, the bending light
                deliver us from evil
and I'm trying to discover who I am
    yet printed there on thinning hair
        I see headlines from court cases
        cold page one bloody presumptions
            of vicious innocence

what will they say about us now
        your parents, the neighbours, our few friends?
    what implied, unanswerable slanders boil
            while police cordon off the area?
    will they be the same words I'm keeping
            secretly, old wounds treasured
            and old compliments festering?
        all the distorted mirrors installed by
            we who could never keep our words
            or rather, kept them and turned them loose

Karen with dead eyes, please look inside me
no one can imagine what I see there
the reflective material in my heart, hard
and seemingly cold, it cannot stop bullets

I regret already
the way imagination fails
and action strips away the flesh
I regret how quickly the gun's heat
faded
the flash flash flash of blue and red lights
the accusation of multiple squad cars
I stashed the rifle
at the back of the closet
and I feel like crawling in after
because what would be the point
in shooting my way out?

remember when we got married, you were the only one
who knew me? Karen only you
could hold the mirror straight and adore me
I was found in Karen
released in Karen
swelling wave, she moved and lifted me
flowed around me and when the tide
turned, she said she would leave
me

you can't go now, Karen
marriage is factory-sealed for our protection
vicious, vacuous cycle that could save
us—broken though we are
stuck spinning on the vast spiral arms
of suburban-as-we-could-afford galaxies
the tires losing traction on slick streets
we slide beyond help

the pain has been real, not as advertised
the denial I wanted, was intolerable
objects in mirror are closer
to reality than they appear

so I sob in the bedroom closet
clutching the rifle and wishing I hadn't
left your body in the parking lot
there's no one to talk to
bereft, nothing to hold

you see, your Honour
classic kindness, a gentle regard
we should honour that, we should keep
cannot allow it to leave
simply find the more appropriate expression
and when hard years burn our hands
we mustn't use words as weapons
as she did, and then discovered silence
a clear escalation in the arms race
she was far better at being quiet
I could never shut up
in that chill, meaningful way
so my recourse was the gun

which buys silence
only for you, my Karen
never quiet for me, never purpose
I never got this much attention before
tonight the television will brandish
domestic dispute goes ballistic
and our adjectives unlaundered
the incoherently collateral damage
our Gulf War syndrome
you were a hardened target
according to my intelligence

## such as it was

you're gonna think I'm whining, Karen
but I miss you
shame-drenched
I've got the haunches shaking, crouched in a corner
holy running shits
I can't hear the megaphone voices
don't answer the counselor's phone call
the brisk shatter of a downstairs window
and the hiss of a tear gas canister
but still I can't, I won't
a cool, sticky feeling spreads over me
the chest wound drying slowly
which can and will
be used against me

## 21 / *Earth from space*

hello, planet
hello, family portrait apparition
    blue island in black vacuum
hello to anything and everything in our grasp

that's Africa in the centre
    a sharp, cloudless image
    her shoreline carved with polished bones
    her deserts like sculpted knives
the other continents, iconic too
    more hidden by clouds and good luck
    though their peculiar shapes are recognized
    instantly, if ever glimpsed without cover
    tagged as homeland, fatherland, heartland
    in hearts educated by maps
    or slantwise recognized as mysterious
    foreign shapes of cultural and ethical
    boundaries, a value-added tax
        on the imagination

in negative space, the oceans our ancestors crossed
    with devices made from the bowels of trees
    perfumed, stained with tar and diarrhea
    emblems in themselves, such vessels
        coracles to tankers
        seed spores, hosts to the virus
        of national pride and transferred value
    sail on, oh ship of nation-state
        mopping bloody discharge from
        a few guns here and there
but from the privileged spaceview the oceans appear
        like absolution
        pure blue forgiveness
        that's why we love this planet

hello, that's me
    in the upper left-hand corner
    somewhat below the horizon
click twice (there's no place like home)
    there we virtually, virally are
        a hotly wired world
    we've spun a web that bears our wait
        in the ether, a necessary place to stand
    we imagine we see the planet below us
        blessed are the moles below the horizon
click twice
    blessed are the meek under the clouds
click twice
    blessed is the summary that we call on
        unconfirmed information age
        knowledge unplanned, aborted rumours
click twice
        Bucky predicted this very image
        would draw us together
        —or was it McLuhan?
        you know...
    a more powerful program could make these
    clouds race together and gather into storms
    which could turn the virtual world on its axis

well yeah, okay
        —escape to the main menu
I should be working, I know, I know

## ♥ / Bottles

the trees toss massive crowns of leaves
    I walk the river road to the beach
an empty styrofoam cup bounces, scumbles
    while thunderheads pile high offshore

let's drink a toast to the birth of philosophy
        all is water
let's smash our glasses on the interzone
        fall down and
        cut ourselves on the rocks
        wash our blood in the ocean
        the salt on salty flesh barely stinging
    because the cold, numbing tides of May
        delete our hisses, our curses
        all that escapes us is a sharp
        take of breath, a small moan

come with me, enter my house
    let us fill each other's mouths with tongue
            come and drink wine
            come watch the rain

do you love to see the river running hard
        meeting the tidal surge?
        where the curve of the beach breaks
        where battling waves never stand?
    the chop is perturbed, neither ocean nor river
        the outcome four times a day uncertain
and after a night's thunder, the piping plover in sunshine
        running/pause/running, leaving no tracks
        no trace in the rain-pounded crust of fine sand
in the storm-spawned surf an empty bottle spins
    liquor broadside, at the mercy of the waves
        jewel-green glass and yellow: Cutty Sark
            can't help wanting to retrieve it
            check for messages

call-forwarding along the Gulf Stream
shake the *Vodou* coffin within

at dusk the tilted moon is a crescent boat upended
the heart a bone-china cup, translucent
and a helicopter flies by overhead
night deepens, waves float above obscurity
appearing as parallel lines in the dark
drawing themselves, erasing them
selves against the unseeable, against
the steady white noise music
braided dragging of sea on land

indoors and a pool of lamplight, two glasses
of wine before I plug in
guitar to amp, amplifier to wall
set the current flowing
the wall outlet looks a little surprised
left vertical slot higher, a raised eyebrow
open mouth, its ground, neutral or disapproving
but the current surges, flows like the ocean
electricity wouldn't say No

touch me as you are cresting and break
ground with me—toes
no longer touching sand
all is water, moist lover, and
whatever ships there are
must sail tonight

## ♣ / The media

robots are perfect television fare
heads like commodities, stock creatures
who obey the magic video wand
(hand me the clicker)
B-9 warns young Will of danger
and Data speaks to Prospero, poses
yet another question about being human

it's impossible to gauge or predict fine entertainment
we just notice the way it sparkles
at a remote control summons
remote and controlling, we are *passe-muraille*
spirits of the micro wavelengths
the passports of radiation surrounding us
our twinkling satellite heaven spins above
and if Caliban doesn't learn to behave
we will cancel his show

everything is television, my child
our words do burn sweet fire upon the hill
by night flames dance across western vistas
by day the brown layer of heat inversion

gesture thus at a screen, the bountiful appears
digits on the automated teller
money like magic in the robot's vest
computers sprouting monitors and keyboards
scanners, voice recognition
a little mouse controls the elephant
(shades of an earlier Disney)
—where DO you want to go today?
and what field are you working in now?
don't kid me, Robert Duncan
how can we sing of the honoured one?
at this grey hour, how do we dance
in fields mined by the pixels of progress?

we are mosquitoes, no more than sparks in the air
tiny appetites approaching, hovering
sustaining the music of desire always
we are not so very hungry, we sing and we rhyme
we want healthy children, pure forms
and our own wild, almost weightless
life principle multiplying...
hold still

oxygen-rich planet, coiled atmosphere of love
where drops of our blood
fly away on wings
what creature, if any, is a vector of disease
when we all tread the sacred mountain?

the sound of another tenant's stereo
creeping up the stairwell, insertions
into private visions, projections
of another's taste, the hoverings in our ears
if a tree falls in the forest
will anyone carry the story?
our enhanced ability to anticipate plot
the full story at eleven, described
in the movement of stars in darker skies
in a world which might dwell behind the eyes

despite which compliant divinity
must mediate—and be mediated
so that you feel your lover's breath against your neck
otherwise what would divine be to us?
feel his breath and know the oxygen burning in his blood
breath of universal fire, sensate cosmic dust
you are his reason
dressed in the skin of intimacy
for being alive this morning

## ♦ / *Money*

hey everybody
let's pump it from the ground and slosh it in the gas tank
beam the stuff through optical fibres
chisel it, shift it to make the great museums
why not trade me some for the value of this book?
your own values adhering to the magnetic strip
I do take plastic
or bauxite, or buttons, strawberries and bombs
diamonds and nickel-steel alloy coins, minted
they bounce through the economy, fall then roll
back to the earth when we loosen our grip

life from out of the earth
garter snakes in a tangle
spilling from the labia
of April-warmed rocks
we use earth magic at a price
the wheat, the lumber
oranges and wine, cotton dresses and hammers
horses, headstones, silicon chips
—the dwarves in the mine drive a hard bargain
all money comes from the earth
but imagine the power, the dominion over all
Dannegeld, property taxes, cottage at the lake
crystal-pure exchange value
we have plans for that money
we can get things done properly
we have a pact with shadows

the spark strangely missing from the eyes of
the once-painted marble heads of state
when you look money in the face
you hardly need to mention poverty
the eyes of hammered stone, polished gold
haunted by absence

the eyes of Geb, Earth-god prostrate
body crumpled into landscape, but straining
every mountaintop stretching
to touch his lost sister-wife, the sky
the eyes make us think of seven lonely dwarves
watching a beautiful sleeper
they cannot waken

we use earth magic at a price
while wheatfields shimmer, shields of hammered gold
we have no choice but to pay
and the myriad of fishes living, gem-like, in the sea

## ♠ / *Wars*

what shall we call our suit of air
    as the eyes launch twin missiles of decision:
        hark the rupture serves us
        hark the rupture owns us
        hark the absolute end of the system
            the sound, the icon—logos hisself

old alchemist, where are my guns?
        and why, hoary magus, have you locked
            all the knives in the cupboard?
        let me use them, let me
            breathe initiation
*why do you want the sword?*
            the master asks me
            to a tune of rats crossing empty streets
        *what is your quest?*

the lush, blessèd mountains exhale our spirit
        while the valleys of the interior are stripmined
            I struggle to name this
I swing unbelayed on frayed rope
        and my hands are sweaty
            with the urge to preach again
        how tempted I am to betray myself
            hyper-charged courage supposing
            what my homeland once was
        these are the cards and they make us
            tremble when we hold them

what I love and whatever I deem
        protectable I have the urge
            to defend with sharpest swords
        savage discrimination
            sharp naming
        that is right
            this is wrong

I have given you my word

yet imagine there exists a purer carving
the cold aloneness of a midnight skater
beyond what we think we know
picture yourself balanced and bladed
sheering light and darkness without judgement
touching diamond ice under moonskies
the swords on our feet are neither magic
nor perfect, but they are transport
through occluded space called Canada
we have the hope of change
we are this bright metal intellect
this fine deity which our trust is
skater's blade, scalpel; and flesh
cleaving as it melds
the new path once unpredicted
a new space for wild mortality

our cat stalks through a pool of streetlight
on the darkened, deserted lane
her eyes are on the pavement
but we cannot see what she sees
then a flash of her claws, snapping
pinning a bit of dark—*why the sword, boy?*
she has something in her mouth
but still we do not see—*what is your quest?*
she takes her prey to the bushes that hem the lane
and when we walk closer
to the place where she disappeared
the cat purrs and begins speaking
from a darkness within the roses:
*oh bring me some boots, young master*
*bring me the very finest of clothing and*
*bring me a sword*

a sword is the way heat melts light
liquifies an image near the horizon
*—to change meaning, Master, then slip away*
*to expose the inner to the outer*
*and to cleave the air*
in one mysterious gap, one strange moment
everything more or less changes
the heart is spliced
the other is added

the warrior's ambivalent identity:
to slice open what you admire
my kitchen knife snips the rose
a blade against an umbilical chord

## The paparazzi as angels of the annunciation

we build the instruments on which to play
    a thousand major chords of cultural conditioning
  the idealized images of men and women
    disguised as specific characters
Blessèd Elvis, Diana, Marilyn, James Dean
    *nous vous supplions à genoux*
  youth, integrity, sexual energy
    all defined by the dead

perhaps the losses and gains reside
    in algebras of characters, Jungian blood types
      of Einstein, Hitler, Chaplin, and Freud
    but icons are beyond representation
      beyond the equal sign of meaning
    they move among us still, godlike
      in their oblique refusal
      to personify much
    metaphors are metaphors
      or something like that

we look through them at
    something else we have no name for
      toying with unresolved
      residues of meaning
    we've been raised by the dead
      no mistake, every generation a fleshy
      link in the dreaming chain gang

hail, ye gods who wear sunglasses
    your sky falls gracefully, gorgeously
      the ground is rushing to a meeting
our surrogate father, who art on television
      hallowed be your program
    give us this day our conventional notions
      a backstage pass to the circus, forget the bread
    and please make Art of our trespasses

as we make Art of those who trespass against us
for evil is to be taken lightly
and being taken lightly is evil

we have forgotten good
—just a synonym for entertaining
fast food for the spirit
and the heart's valves clogged
we've become the ghost in the commodity
tragic family of *passe-muraille* trapped
within walls of images
we thought to consume
images of beauty and courage
selves choked in a span of stone

# Pinball

the Bally Company in 1933
came out with an early pinball game
called Rocket
and players could win cash, a rattlespew of coins
if the score was high enough
New York City said it was gambling
and therefore illegal
LaGuardia made political points by smashing
a wicked machine with a sledgehammer
while the press watched
so the rival Gottlieb Company invented flippers
and the free game, free continuation
awarded to the skilful, well-practised player
the new machines were legit
made even more money
everyone was happy
may the shrewdest signifier win

during World War II, it is said, both sides
used crossword puzzles in the propaganda war
planes dropping leaflets to be solved
over civilian target areas
a German puzzle might ask:
what's a nine-letter word
for "warmonger"
with clues that prompted the player
to answer: "Churchill"
and so it goes
in stories, songs, poems and paintings
of war, wealth, freedom
and pornography
the old intractables seem to beg
for a tweak of the public mind
beg for the hubris once again
to create and/or disturb

the anciently balanced appetite
tilt the moral axis with poetry
because the dreaded hammer will soon fall
a hammer which we fondle, barely grasp

talk of simply joy
and that will make the beauty sooner accused
a wasted verbal effort
on the front lines
yet the white spaces leap out
the possibility of inscription
—I love new dreams
and music never heard by human ears
bring me to the edge of Eden, please
I need a glimpse of what I'm fighting for
give me falling, flailing ecstasy
capture of the soul headlong
in beauty's nets, and let me invent
an I                    ...to do the falling
but retrieve me from sirens at the last minute
block my ears with bullets
remind me of the real world

thank you, comrades, for bringing me home
to the war—I got so woozy bouncing
between Lotus land and No Man's land
sex and tear gas and rock 'n' roll
throw cold water, brothers and sisters
on whatever music I play
fire words cruel enough to destroy all art
smash my head against the wall of justice
just grant us, please, one unfettered vision
before I bow under meaning

# Editorial judgement

yet another poem on the instability of text
or reviewing the sense of an ending
not always beginning and middle and
somewhere between Kermode Ave
and the Isle of Patmos
I wuz prepositioned by a lady

'twas a strong angel, proclaiming in a loud voice
'cross the slip vector of St John's Revelation
*Who,* she sez, *is worthy to open the book*
*and to loose the seals thereof?*
so I had a quick peek at this Book of visions
which seems to be a Vision of books pre-deconstructing
themselves before disassembling
the world they sit in the womb of
who indeed, I thought
ducks judgement and the eventual
transfiguration of definite articles
who beats the proteins of intellect re-folded
by linear and plutonic seeing which requires
a faithful copy, transparent
bid for safety avec sameness
time meeting parchment in a dead stop
ignoring the faithlessness copying implies

something about the historical moment when scrolls
gave way, flapping like cartoon windowblinds
replaced in a re-twist of the helix and
a codex arrives, oblique like muscle tissue
tectonic tilt of sedimentary technology
revealed in, edited by, noticeably eroded
no longer were stories the same swirls of law
and prophecy and history raked into piles
of dry papyrus leaves tumbled in a corner
a curse was the threshhold of the codex

John closing heaven's door on any editor
who dared change a word in the text
adding words, he says
*shall add unto him the plagues*
*that are written in this book*
and deleting words
*shall take away his part*
*out of the book of life*
THE END
the original codex moment
flash frozen and bound

and a voice from the chair saith unto me
(I can't really say throne since I've never
seen an actual "throne" and to most of us
such things are a vague mythology—so
let's translate this as...)
and a voice from Dad's favourite chair saith unto me
*Write*
—I'll do my best
*These are the true sayings of God.*
—who am I to argue?
Don't you ever mess with my scriptures
—wouldn't dream of it
and in time the book will be fulfilled
(as long as nobody screws up the text
we'll know exactly what's coming)
thus ends the great age of Scripture...

a book is hinged like a well-made door
swinging softly open
dropping swiftly closed
transmission is a parable
—and he that overcometh all flaws in a text
I will write upon him
my new name

I will give him
    the morning star

    and the globe, national edition

# Voyage ton flag

*Il y a des fois je me sens tout seul dans ma musique.*
—Dennis McGee, Cajun fiddler, age 90

for fiddlers who opened a village barbershop
for fisherman fiddlers and workers at the feedstore
for the fiddles always priceless on a bachelor's bedroom wall
and nothing beyond repair, fiddles rising from the dead
and especially for the young person's improvised, wish-filled
first fiddle handcarved by his callous, youthful hands
from a wooden cigar box, tobacco-scented even now
then carefully the wire unwoven from the back window screen
wire for the four strings to the bridge, man, an' out the door

something handed down now gives him passion for the sound
he's got to spend every copper penny, his patience and hard pluck
gathering long horse hairs for the rosin-scented bow, and
through the night fog, the old dance hall
tumbles notes in his hand

chanky-chank before recordings were made
boy, you know you're damn poor
when you toss out old *grand-père* things, buy the first tractor
ever seen in these parts—hey, Hank Williams and Henry Ford
were foreigners *en Louisiane* and the Monarch accordion
those accordions from the catalogue
the Monarch accordion was a cross-cultural influence

*le Reel du pendu*, the cotillions and mazurkas
all the old-time dances from a century ago
have all but passed away, except for tunes in the fiddler's head
it only stays a living culture until the last fiddler dies

*les contredanses* and the rounds, oh the lancers people danced
tell me, *jeunes 'Cadiens*, when you come back to your homes
as folklore collectors, like hungry young consumers

do you come home like the prodigal to play your two-steps
and your waltz?

if Americans love the Cajuns now, or if any of us the "white trash"
it's for the sake of our displacement, sense of loss we feel firsthand
old Longfellow made a myth-world, made a romance out of war-crime
but most of us only know this life, know we never get what's gone

to be walking the plank floors of a musical, sweet life
booted feet that were tapping dust in the shade of someone's porch
no artists and no art forms, just the dances handed down
—it's not the meaning of the words, it's the meaning of the sounds
it's not the meaning of the words
(drama of the untranslatable)
it's not the meaning, or the words
it's defiance, a state of exile
our rhythm is never the sound
of otherness to ourselves

chanky-chank in the record shops at the global village mall
are there artists, are there art forms, is there money handed down?
the old dance halls, through
the night fog, tumble
notes in-
to our hands

## Courting disaster

the twinkling stern of the ship lurches skyward
a floating erection, a black star
apartment building in ice water
the leaning tower of vanity
and mad explorers, we plunge deeper into Amazonia
Murphy's law kicks over Chernobyl, spreading the fire
which deftly illuminates the Hindenburg
—remember to diversify your holdings

I am a HAL 9000 series computer
I am the Berlin Wall and forked lightning
enough volcanic ash to fertilize an island
I am the Nile
your rent money has been invested in a pyramid scheme
the rich and the powerful have already fled
this is a love poem
—what colour is your parachute?

rewriting our Notes from Underground, I've been keeping
a worm's-eye view on old Brother Noah
from my spot at Merlin's Bait Shop
a wave of sane proportions is called desire
more than we can handle is called love
love, oh my love , walk through those swinging doors tonight
I want you to sing like a bird, drink like a fish
kiss me and don't untie the boat
when you rock it, unless you really
need that sense of purpose you get
when swept out to sea with no oars

luck is with me, far across
this harbour of grapes and hops
I see the goddess coming
the pulse in her wrists is swift
like a sparrow in the hand, she's
an urban raccoon mother, prowling and restless

her breasts inside her shirt are live wires
shock therapy
there's a spell for this; I'm sure I knew it once
I had dreams with no edges, they blended
with conjuring, but I try wishing
I think: say hello, take a chance with my eyes
there's plenty for breakfast back at my place
and all time was constructed, invented just for you
for that moment when you walked in the room

once upon an evening there was a famously horizontal ship
floating and winking her flirtatious lamps at the sea
music bursting from her seams
champagne on ice
like a fool, I'm sailing on but won't cry out for mercy
from the tongues of ice that sooner or later
fellate every gambler, every drowning sailor
who pulls off his shoes in lascivious haste

although I might try prayers or a plea for apocalypse
temporary suspension of old cause and effect
all that I ask is this one bet
be not determined by the last
cautious lover, come home with me tonight
all is lost
all is forgiven

## The mission of the secular heart

rounded and deep-set red
pointing in, yet pointing out
like buttocks, like cleavage above
and crimson tip below
someone took my heart away
a hungry heart
a lonely heart
a broken heart
two hearts beating as one

crying her heart out
his heart was in his mouth
lifting up our hearts
our hearts pounding
someone took your heart away...
could this belong to you?
I think you forgot it last night
and which lies covered at the heart of love?
what's covered by growing intimacy?
desire: the expanding romantic economy
a doctrine of growth
love conquers all
out-performs the competition
survivors are blossoming everywhere
their allergies bothered
by dust from the rubble

two sheets of red construction paper
some paper lace glued at the edges
I pledged my heart
stapled down the sides
open at the top to receive
valentines and invective
the scratch on my hand
from a bent staple

and don't suppose, sweetheart
when we enter each other's hearts
all the weeping will be over
no simple exchange of fluids
of blood-siblinghood, will do
patterns of blood course through muscles
convulsing the hormonal self to energy
—we are neural networks
and I will take you to my heart
which is
in the body

oh honest my love, the blue gaze you recall
photos of your face in spring light and
each of our bodies held in memory
the only kinds of icons that matter

## Her *handful of stars flung*

there was one particular late night
that I remember
Bronwen Wallace, Ingrid de Kok and I
discussing our homes and emigration
old roots of belonging and not belonging
Bronwen saw mostly the romance of exile
of being pushed out of countries by ideas
while Ingrid denied this was much fun at all
and a deep connection to Kingston
being a local, like Bron
was better, meant more
now the memory of Bronwen is a candle
carried inside of us
Ingrid is back in South Africa, and I
cross the Thousand Islands Bridge
again on a hot August day
mere embroidery on the interzone

and they say everything becomes personal
eventually
every song and vision, every child conceived
announced by human voices
even the unreal of the media, must
somewhere, beyond airwaves, walk into kitchens
pour the coffee and make the toast
so our time on earth is a pair of bent glasses
the spokes of an old wheelchair, a stone
thrown at the head—anything that touches

I remember wishing for a star who could
change the world, wishing for many
Che Guevaras, John Lennons
but then the great circle of women, with their arms
bared, pulled the tree of heaven out
by the roots, to reveal we were living in clouds

mythologies ourselves, revelling in illusions
blind always, we float in the Mother's hand
all the nations like cell cultures bathing
in returning waves of amniotic fluid
the world is unchanged or ruined
depending on who you've been reading

the heavenly stars are only people, Bron might say
friend of the heart, walking across the sky
we all have dreams of starfire, ambitions
want ancient metaphysical laws
bent to our sacred whims
we dream a planet made of cinnamon and nutmeg
our bare feet flying off the ground
our sleeping spouses and children abandoned
like cats curled up on the radiator
while we travel soul and body high over the world
our very footsteps igniting plasma fire
our mere substance becoming real
nine lives trailing behind us, condensed
into one simmering moment of illumination

Bron, you had a way of addressing us
directly in a poem, speaking out
from the heart and belly with one more glass
of Bluebird wine
in your poetry we see traces of
*that widening of the wild zone*
*between the power to fight what happens to us*
*and the power to accept what is*
but what happened in your case is our longing
our leaning towards you and the piece
of sky you travelled in as you were
led away, swapping stories as you went
the lasting image of you, trailing kitchen beauty
your most graceful poems held in place

by fridge magnets and the lonesome sound
of Emmylou Harris
you taught us, older sister, made us listeners
to the dumb speech of sorrow in a million
homes, to the solemnity of working prayers

now, you are walking across the sky
stopping here and there to heave
great holes in heaven's floor
to let through the smell of horses and gardens
smoke of sacred herbs, smell of fresh bread
and the sheets of illness, bruises of abuse
I'm sure you won't want me getting too sentimental
making an angel of you and placing you
everywhere at once, watching us all
you're too busy to watch, I imagine
giving the galaxies a push, so they'll
slowly turn, putting your spin on
all the stars and calling it revolution

come on, Bron, you can tell me
is this the best we can hope for?
that little spark that arcs across
the bitter space between life and memory?
the action, the brief flicker of movement that serves
as an inspiration to make things happen
when we're gone?    is that all we can have?
I would much rather hope for    really hearing you speak
from your wildzone    the skyish world that must be there
hear your actual voice    from the place that lies between
memory    and poems

## Shining threads

imagine
a bubble-pack envelope arrives in the mail, addressed to you
        inside you find a small evergreen bough
            fir or cedar: delicate cones, gentle needles
        and a brightly coloured condom, packaged
            tightly furled in see-through wrapper
            and something you wouldn't have bought
            because it's red and silly, or green
            banana-flavoured, or shimmy-down blue
        here it is
            the anonymous gift, no return address
                but you have your suspicions

tenses have become confusing
        you don't have time for that
everybody's talking about icons, but
        they don't know the meaning of the word
        it's nobody's business and every kind of business
            shakes its tail on the circuit these days
                —everything except invisible mending

dark embroidery, metallic thread on velvet
    loop of silver on green
        the dancers are in the barley corn
    you inch past the dream of whetted sickles
        by insisting on herbal remedies
    one should never say essence, say
        greener energy
        a velvet curtain of tides
        lunar/solar dipolar
      say
        the broken O
        the holy abalone
        church of the blessed vulva
        locked in a span of red

it's in the blood
embroidered with protein thread
conjugating you, the verb

somewhere Hakim Bey quotes a "Bishop Hoeller"
as saying consciousness, rather than raw materials
and physical resources, constitutes wealth today
therefore, the mastery of consciousness
in other words control of information...
I don't even want to think about this
like Hakim, I won't believe
in the triumphal bit stream
in the future Information Wars
if power really comes to that
are to be scorned as lies

and if it comes to your stubborn, bless'd body
both the parts with hair
and the places that gleam
then imagine the guidance of our hands
the not-struggle of our senses
when it comes to your stubborn, bless'd body
imagine me saying:
did you get my message?

## Hunting for wild paradigms

you, prince of fools, hunting for that liberty tree
we decree you outside the institution
as you wish, your legitimacy is questioned
and for egregious independence of mind
we allow that issues of sanity
will dog your heels, you crazy bastard

off you go then
nature's child by a previous marriage
hunting the rebellious paradigms
digging that crazy wilderness, man
inside out, lost and found
wondering if icons are made, not
born and outed

puzzling whether creation is endless
endlessly boring, endlessly
corruptive/eruptive, endlessly
living, endless creative flow
of the endless original blessing
and otherwise God
her queendom never stops, just jars
our attention spasm span
across such indelicate absence

blessèd true authenticity, tent-city university
let us imagine that we are close to death
in avant-garde gear we move
purposeful, trekkers on Everest's West Ridge
longing for oxygen, feeling
the cold winds of new metaphor
and mourning our comrades crushed
in the icefalls below
somehow we never understand, don't have the words
until we grow them, push them
out through black and white gardens

rearing them on crystal display flat
lit screens synaptic video suspension
powerbook passageways in the brain

I will quest-shun the tendon-sea of reality before you do
because my mean, hardwired lowdown
unconscious is better than yours
—I will beat you to the hunch, scholar
I will look at the back of your hands, how they knurl and
pucker, each distinctively as we both
settle down, finer hairs, fluff-eared
crinkled sensitivity, carpetbags below the eyes and
lift up thy blood overpass unto the Lord
hand's wrinkled demonstration of vein and bone

wish us luck, children, we're making our bid
to solve all the riddles, enter the city of light
this very year, flags of midnight rent
and cracking, wind whistling in our ribs

speaking of which, through my jawbone I hear music
like a dentist's drill—Puccini sort of
drawn out slowly, until the end moment
of powerful intensity is a taffy-pulled
single high note dying away
the languid steel of Eden
oh sail me across the bay
across the cove of the world
to the smell released from a rotten tooth
smell of humid forest floors in autumn
smell of decaying timbers in the sieve-like
basements of nineteenth-century limestone
Kingston walls propagating centipedes and
propping up the slumlord's myopic cash machine
and sound released finally from the ferry's bow in spring
tinkling, crushing concert with every crossing

iceblink in loose light waves over warm white
and sound bunching in damped surges before longer days
the fluid promise of warmth—old sun's off her leash
black glasses, bicycle shorts, robins returning
the tapestry of blue-eyed flowers on the lawn
and our heavy coats open to the wind
who needs radar to spot the geese, locate renewal
find the crow in the pines, sense
the humid roll of lakeward air, released?

all the wilderness we ever need
crashes daily
through the seven gates of the body

oh gods and goddesses in the details
sail me, skim me like a fat, flat stone
a vat of nervous laughter crossing this harbour
and a ship without cargo, destiny or home